Good Enough to Eat

Still Life Trompe l'Oeil

N.P. James ROI

Cv /Vi s ual Ar t s Re s e a r c h Series 204

Good Enough to Eat
Still Life Trompe l'Oeil

ISBN 978-1-910110-18-8

Cv/Visual Arts Research Series ISSN 1476-9980

Printed and bound by
Blissett: Design.Print.Media
www.blissettdigital.co.uk

Cv Publications
www.tracksdirectory.ision.co.uk

Good Enough to Eat

The series of trompe l'oiel still life watercolours was made from 1978-80 and first exhibited as 'Good Enough to Eat' at Dodo Old Advertising West London in November 1978. Further commissions by Gilbert/Robinson inc. Kansas spread the series across the United States with large scale marine paintings featured in the company's Bristol Bar and Grill chain. Subjects such as *The Strawberry* alone gathered $10,000 revenue from prints, proving its wide popular appeal. In 2014 the artist has permitted a new edition of twenty studies scanned from originals in private collections. The catalogue is one of three published in February 2015 which feature different aspects of the artist's repertoire.

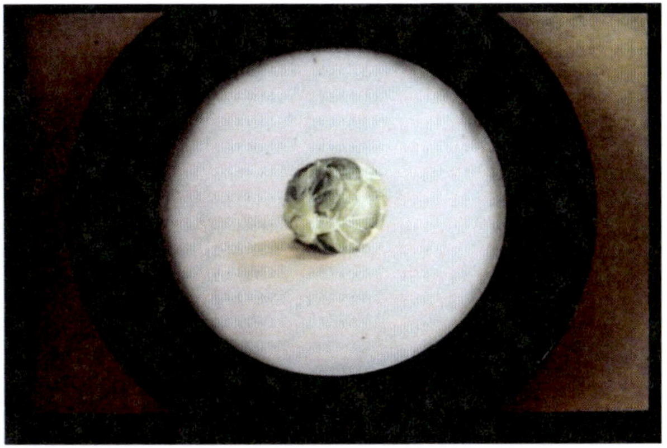

Brussel Sprout 1978
Watercolour and gouache on Ingres paper 5″ x 5″
Private Collection

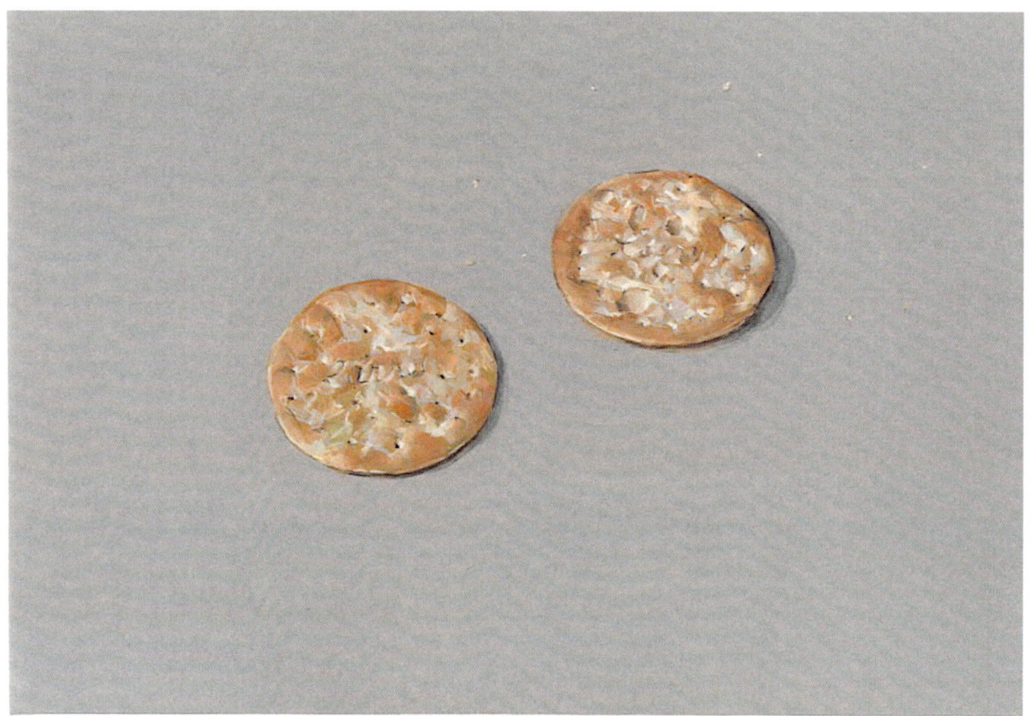

Water Biscuits 1980
Watercolour and gouache on Ingres board 7″ x 11″
Private Collection

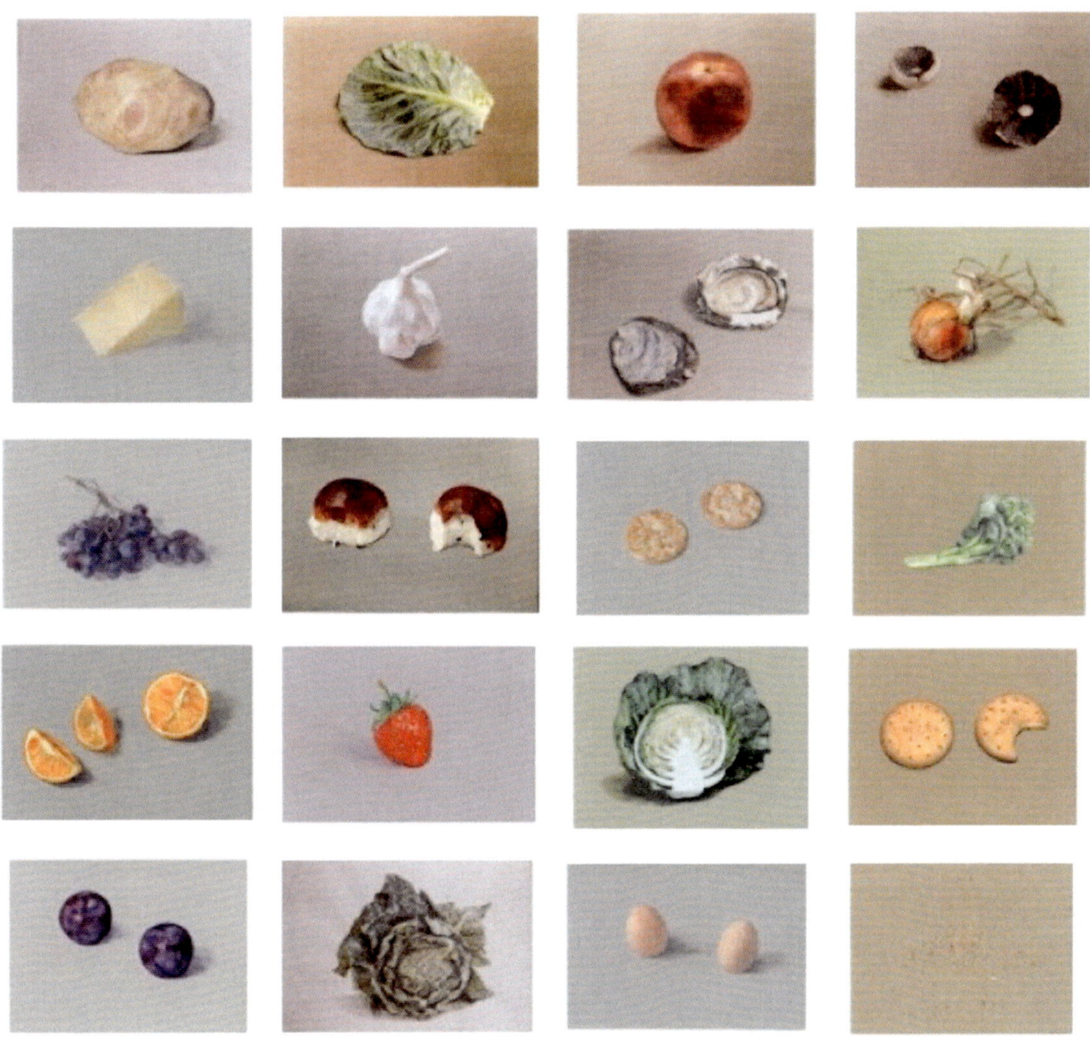

Good Enough to Eat 1978-81
Watercolour and gouache on Ingres board 7″ x 11″
Private Collection

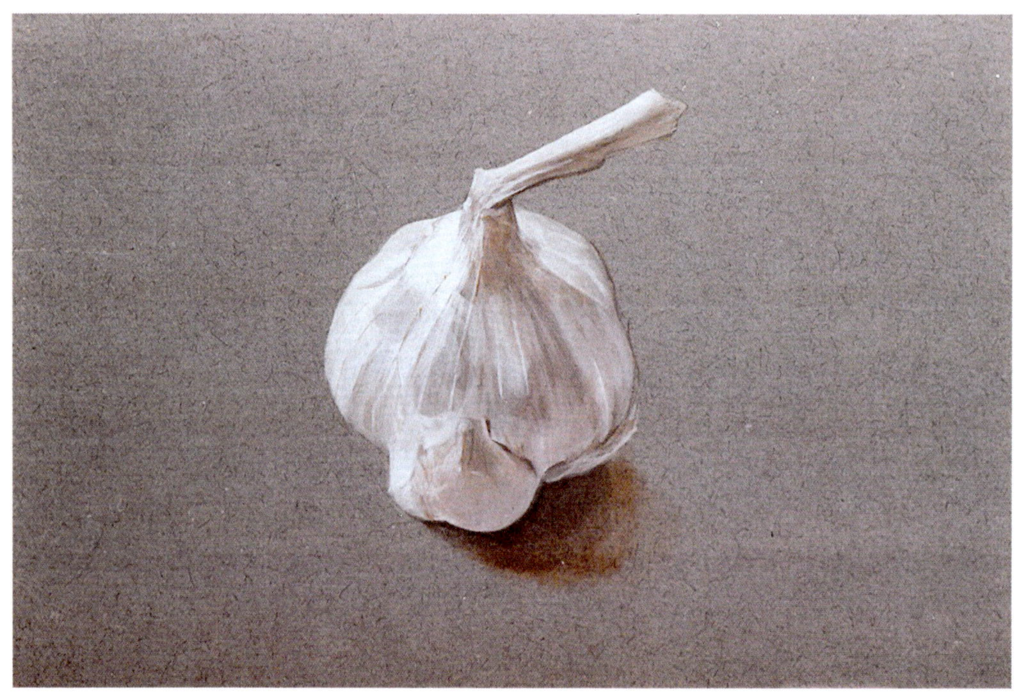

Garlic 1980
Watercolour and gouache on Ingres board 7″ x 11″
Private Collection

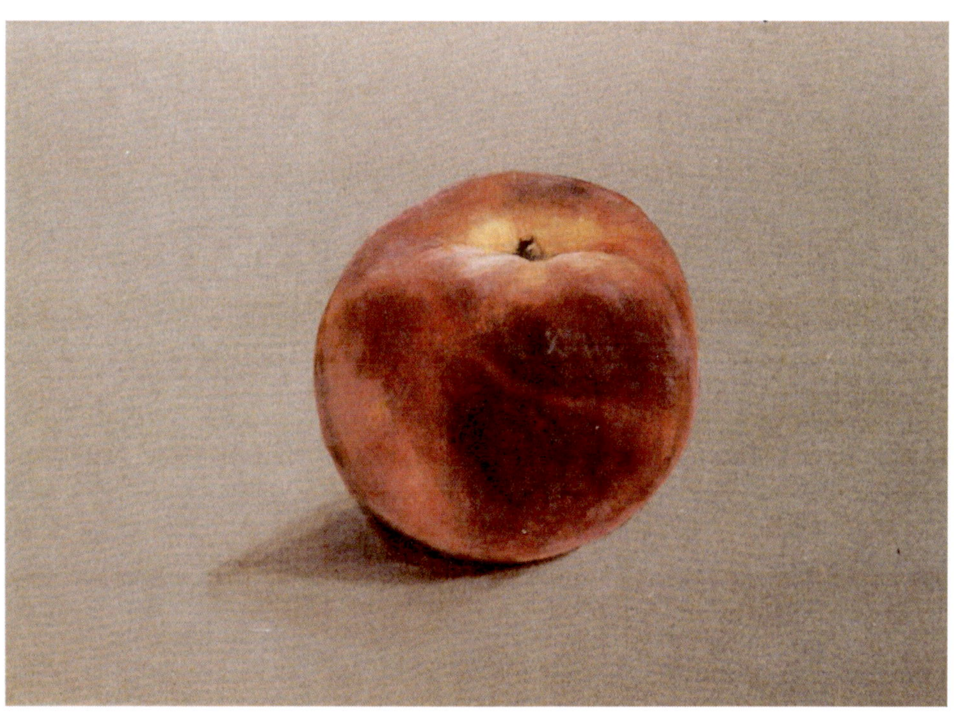

Peach 1978
Watercolour and gouache on Ingres board 7″ x 11″
Private Collection

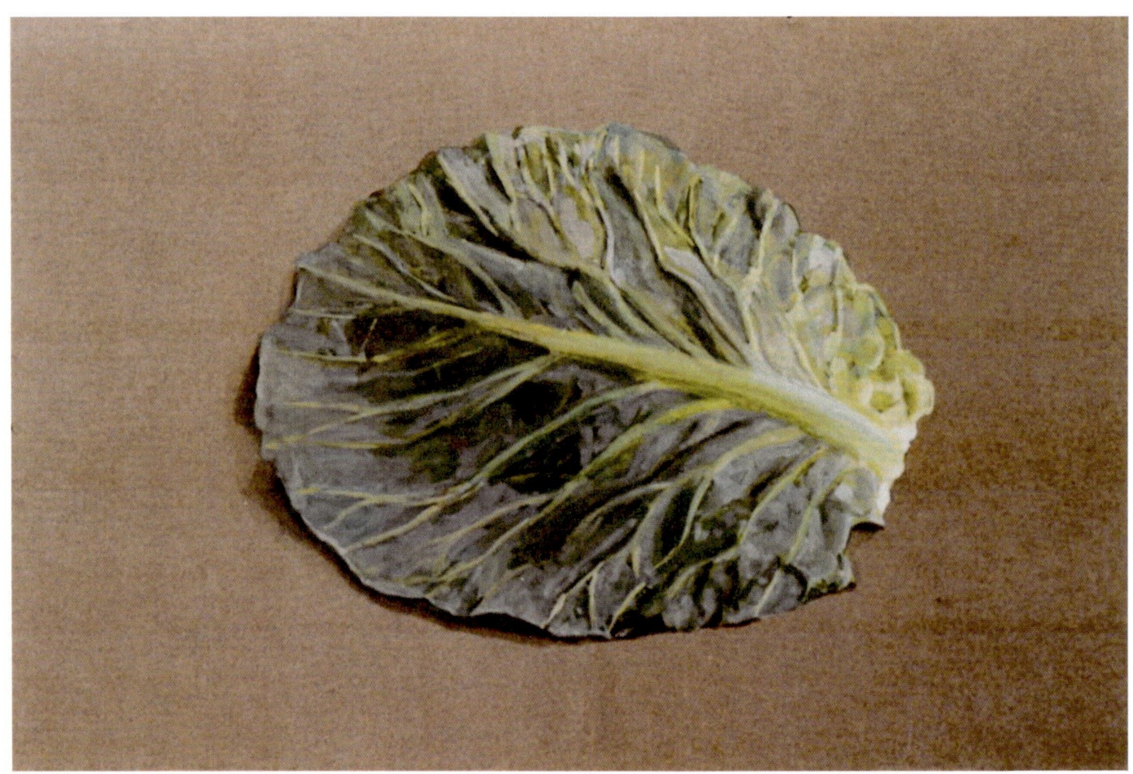

Cabbage Leaf 1978
Watercolour and gouache on Ingres board 7″ x 11″
Private Collection

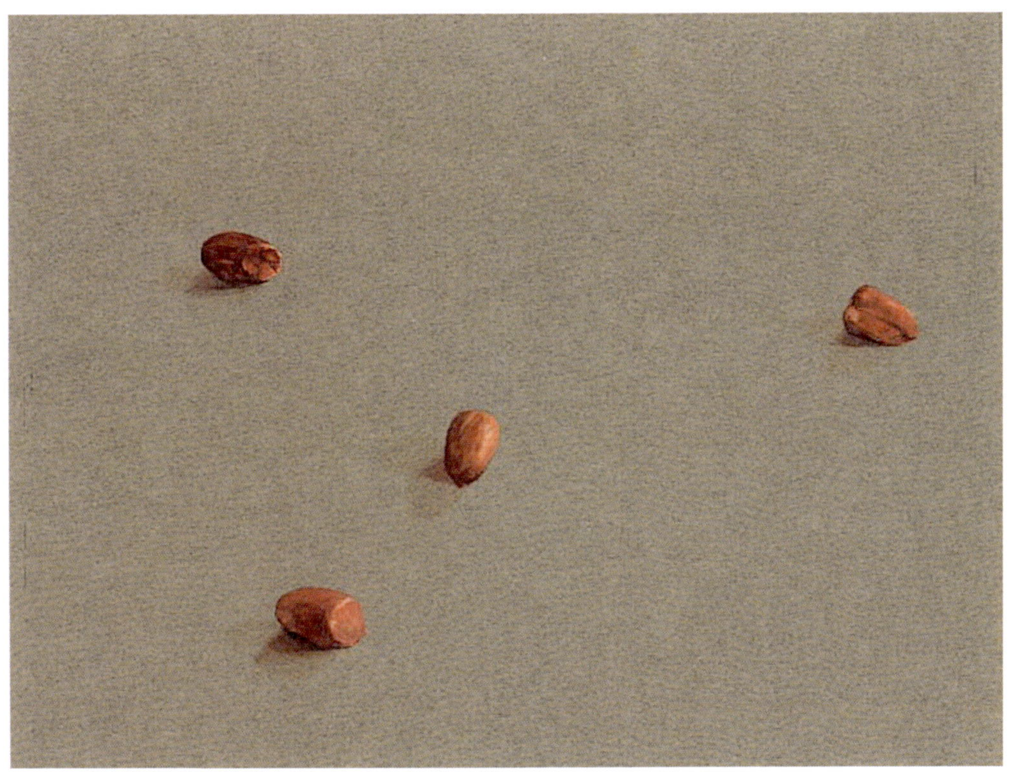

Hazelnuts 1980
Watercolour and gouache on Ingres board 7″ x 11″
Private Collection

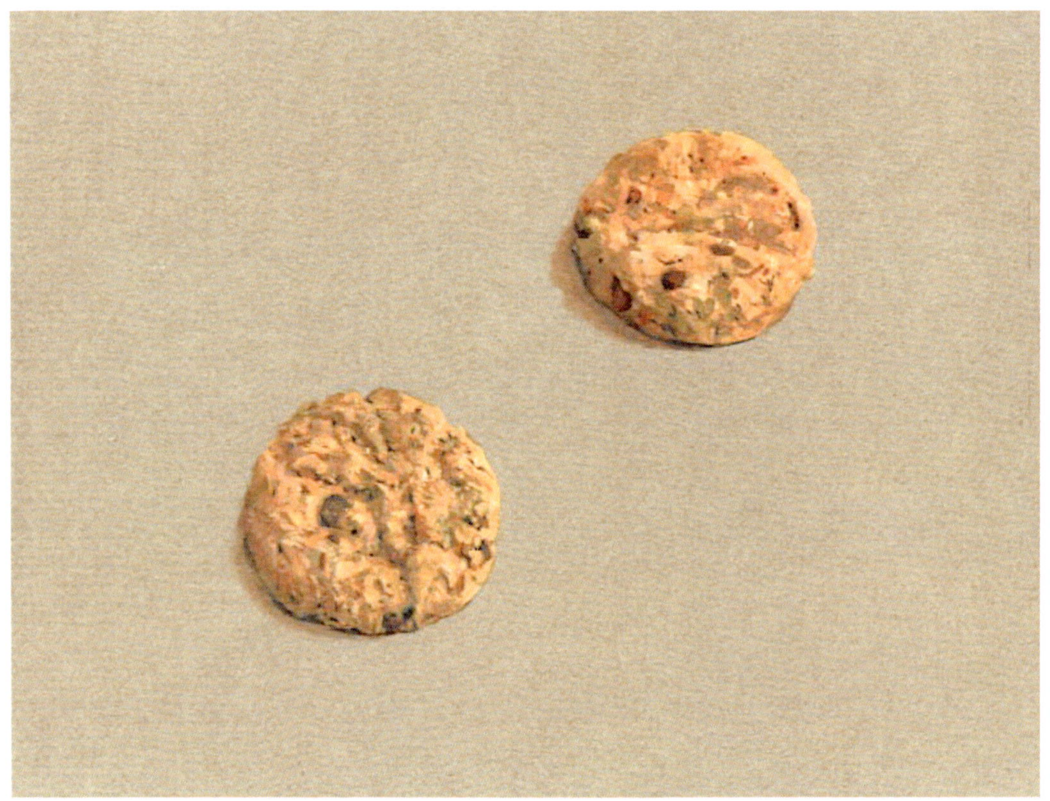

Cookies 1978
Watercolour and gouache on Ingres board 7″ x 11″
Private Collection

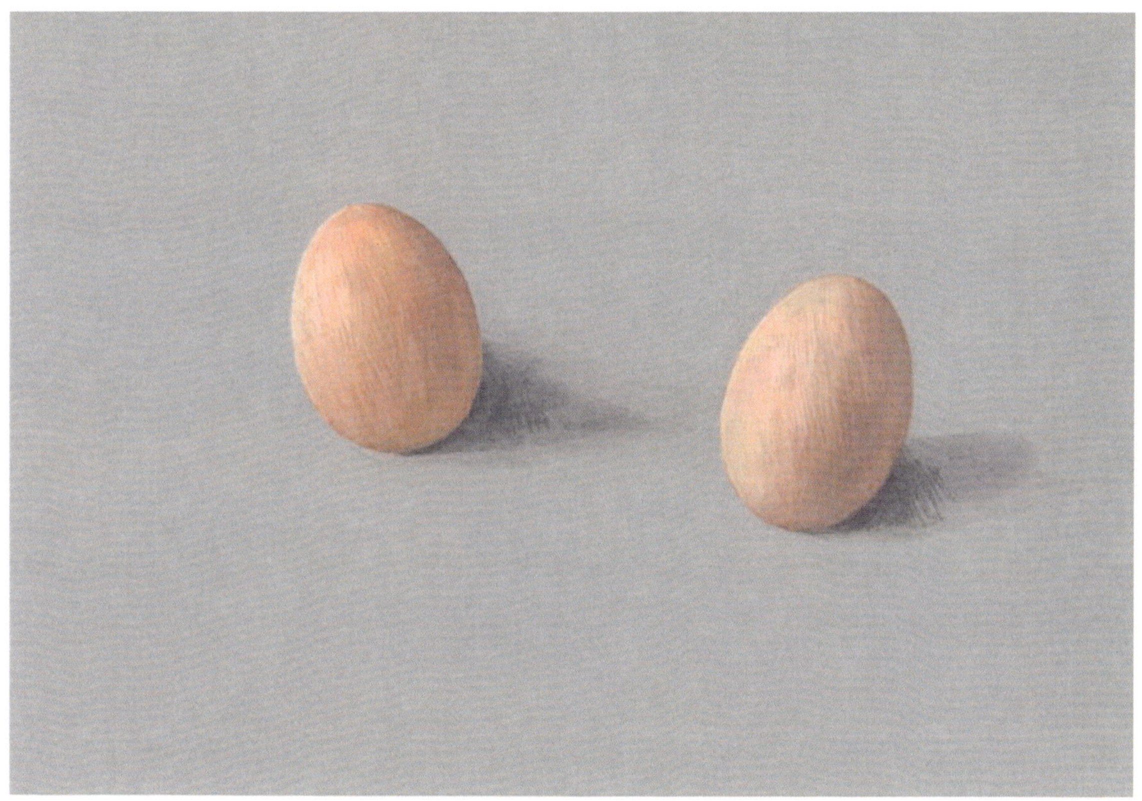

Eggs 1980
Watercolour and gouache on Ingres board 7″ x 11″
Private Collection

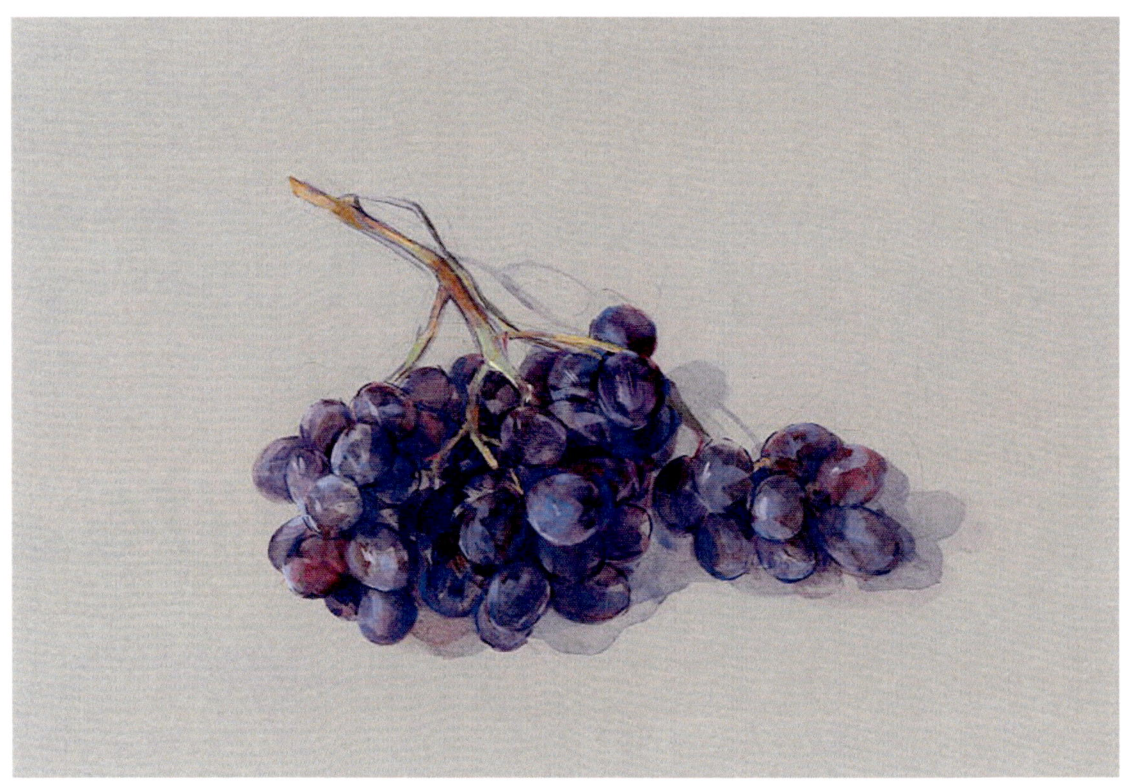

Black Grapes 1980
Watercolour and gouache on Ingres board 7″ x 11″
Private Collection

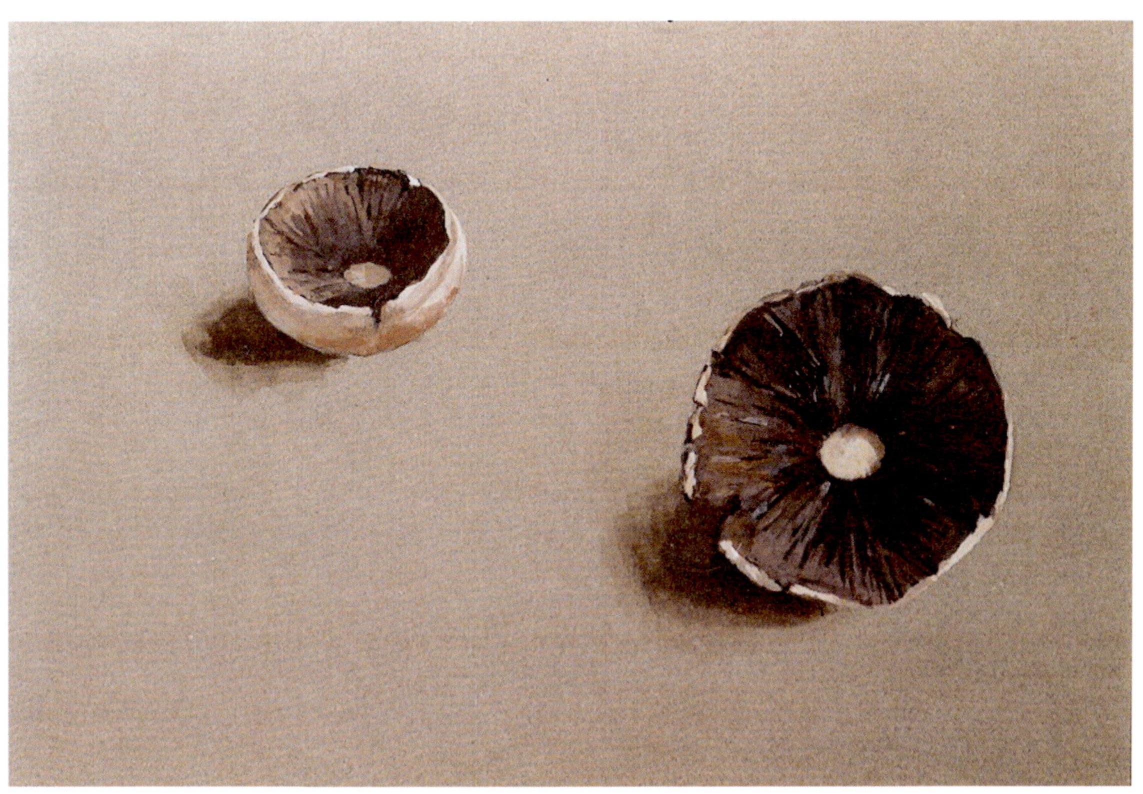

Mushrooms 1978
Watercolour and gouache on Ingres board 7″ x 11″
Private Collection

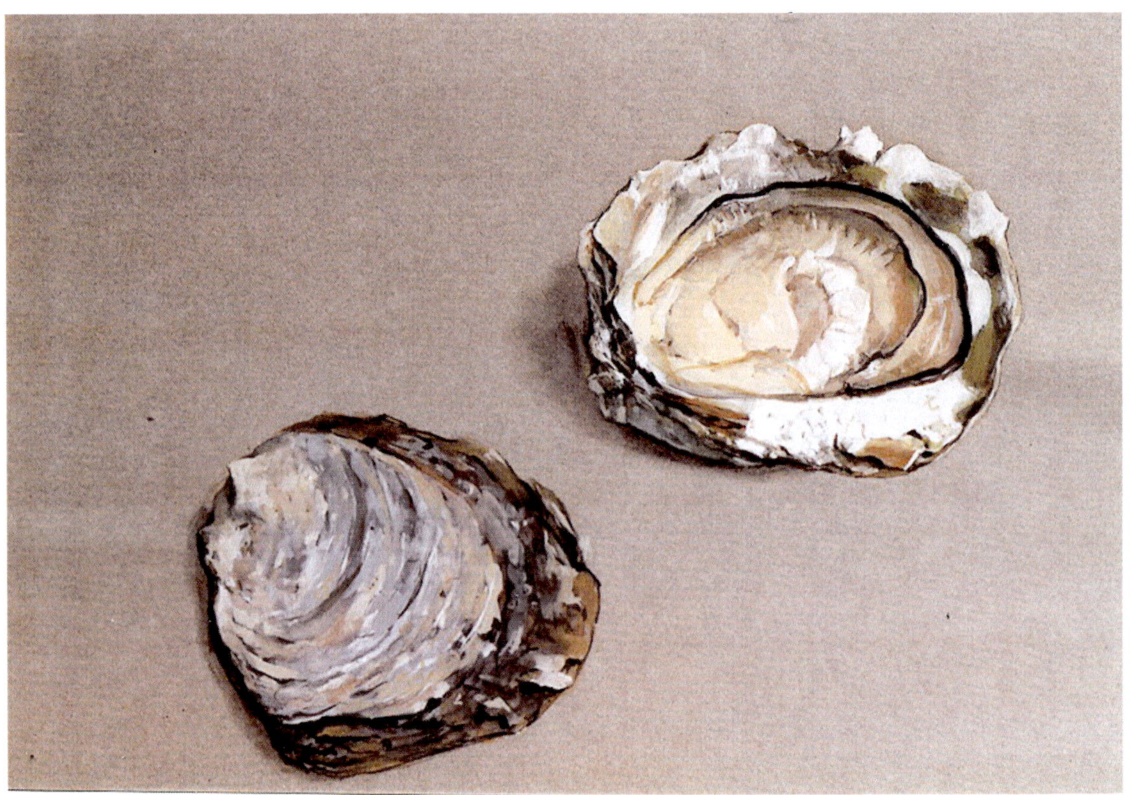

Oyster 1979
Watercolour and gouache on Ingres board 7″ x 11″
Private Collection

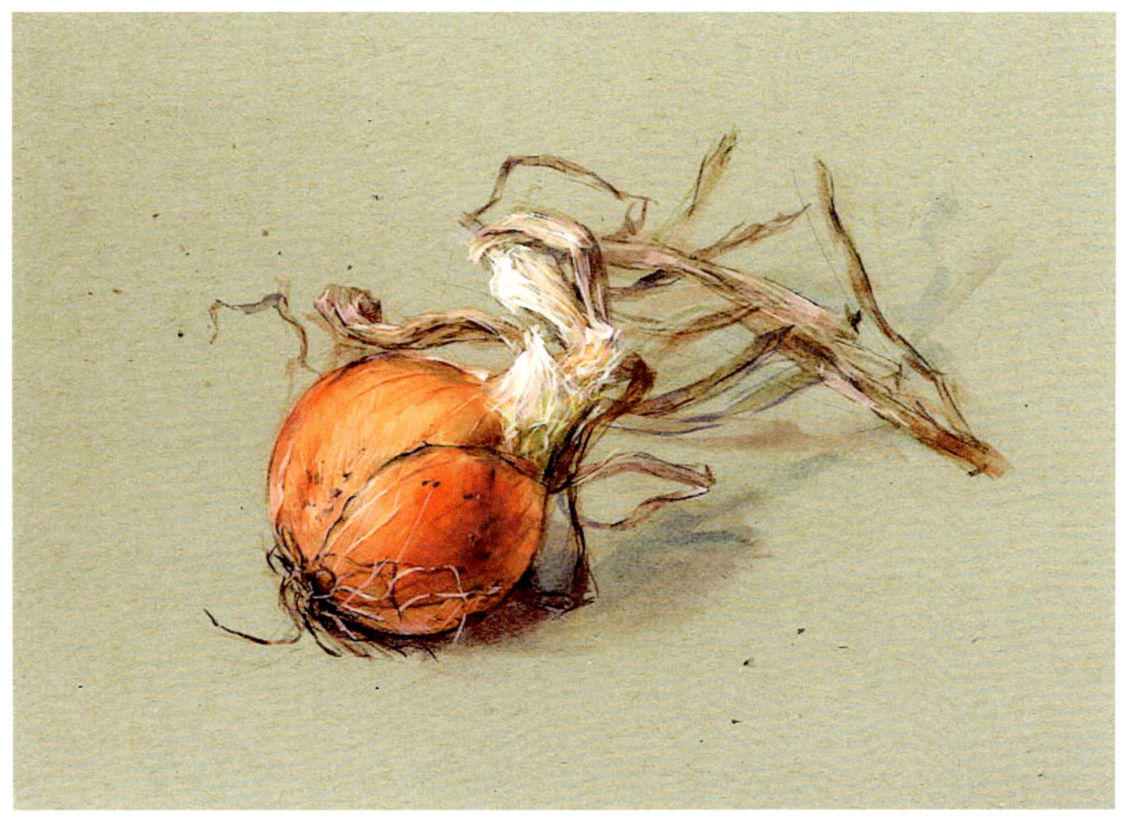

Onion 1980
Watercolour and gouache on Ingres board 7″ x 11″
Private Collection

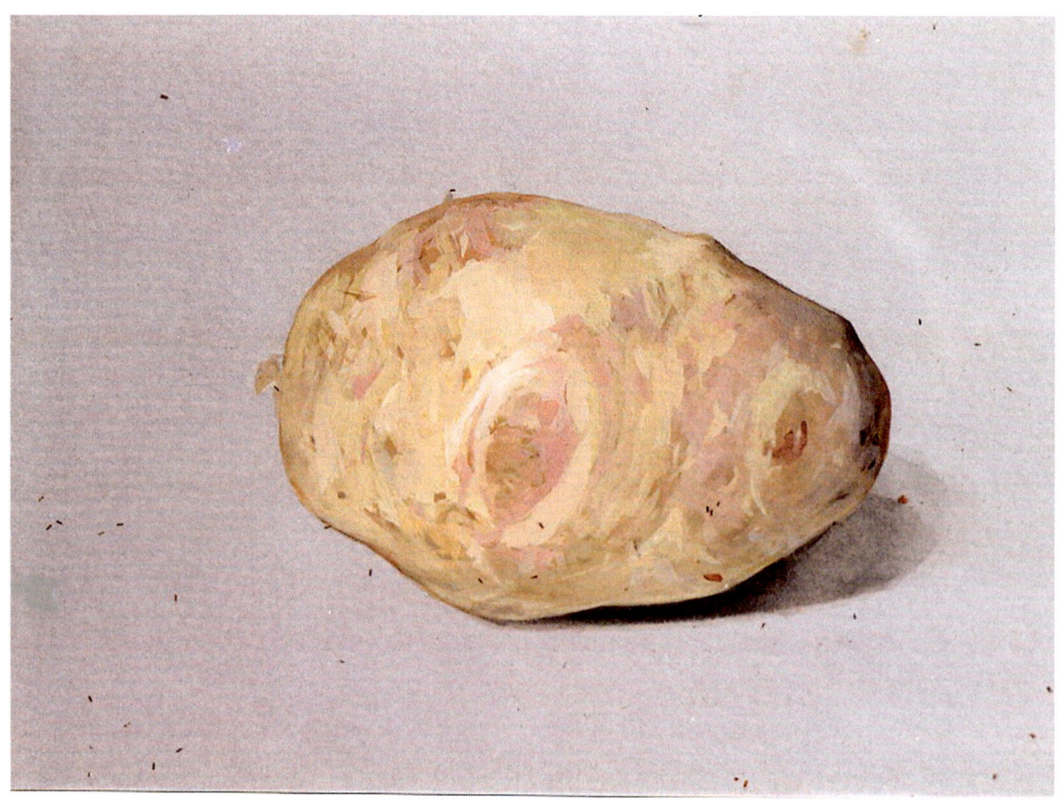

Potato 1980
Watercolour and gouache on Ingres board 7″ x 11″
Private Collection

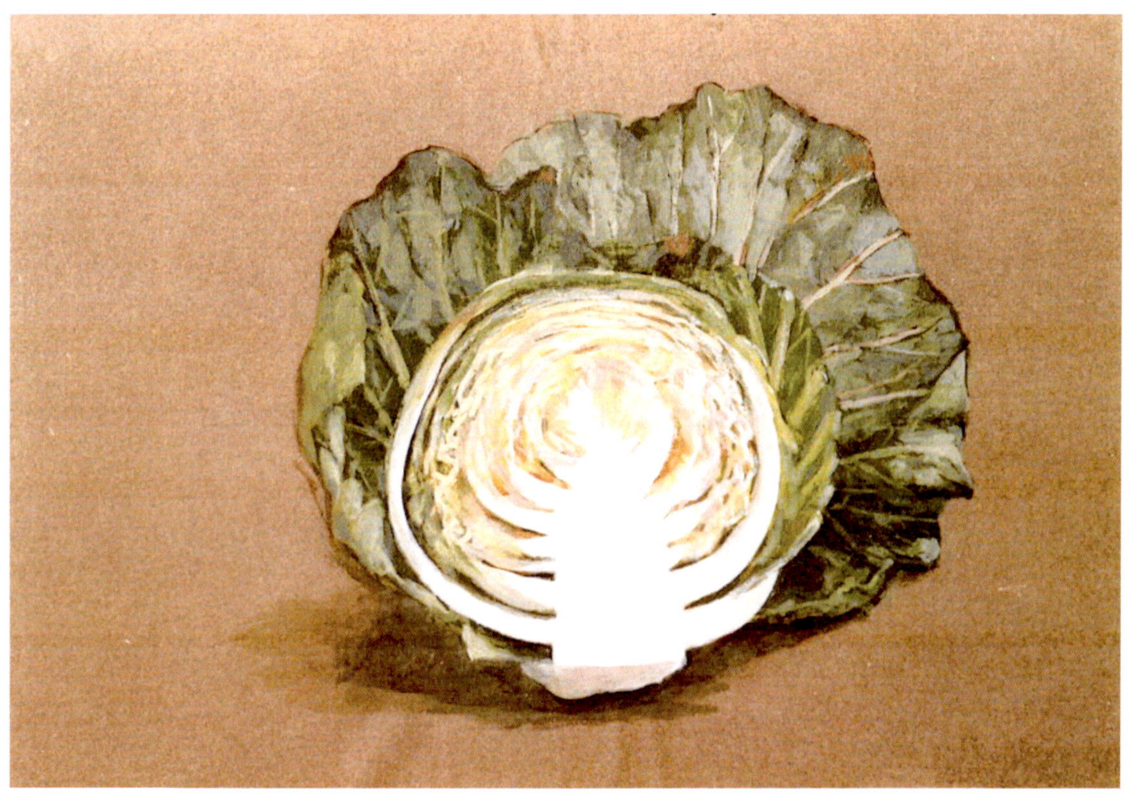

Half Cabbage 1978
Watercolour and gouache on Ingres board 7″ x 11″
Private Collection

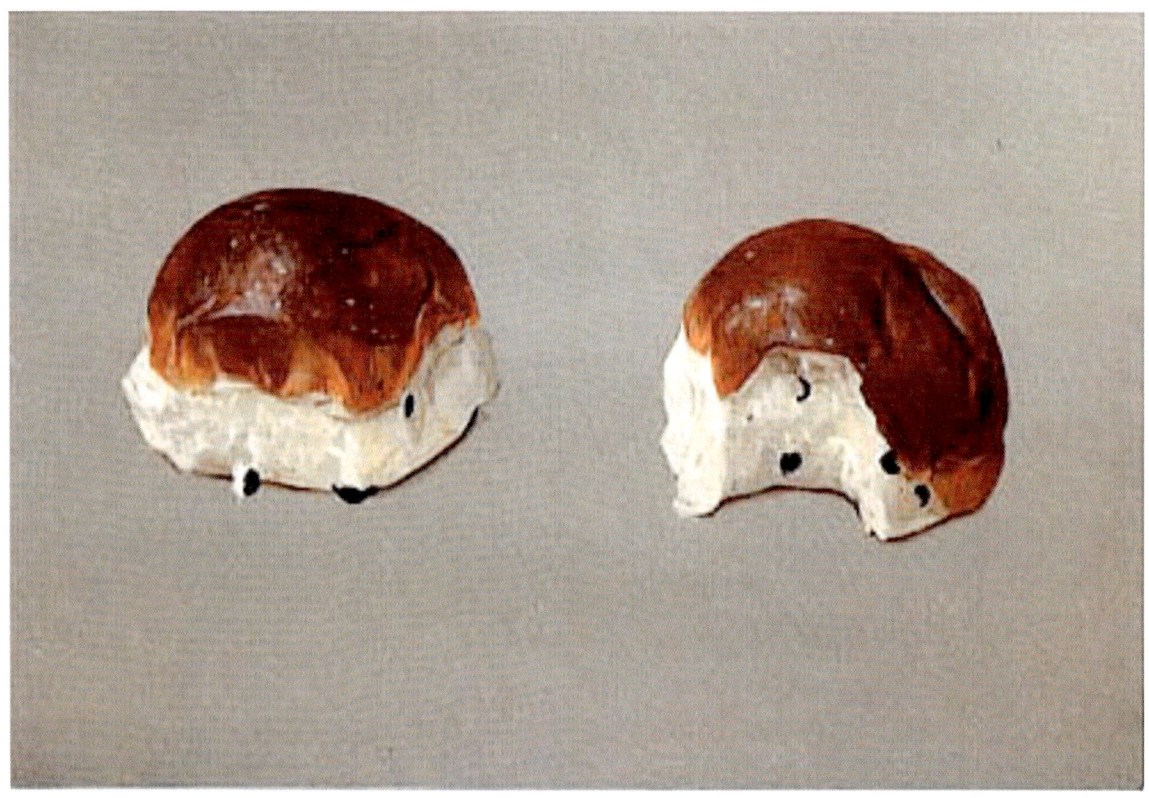

Buns 1980
Watercolour and gouache on Ingres board 7″ x 11″
Private Collection

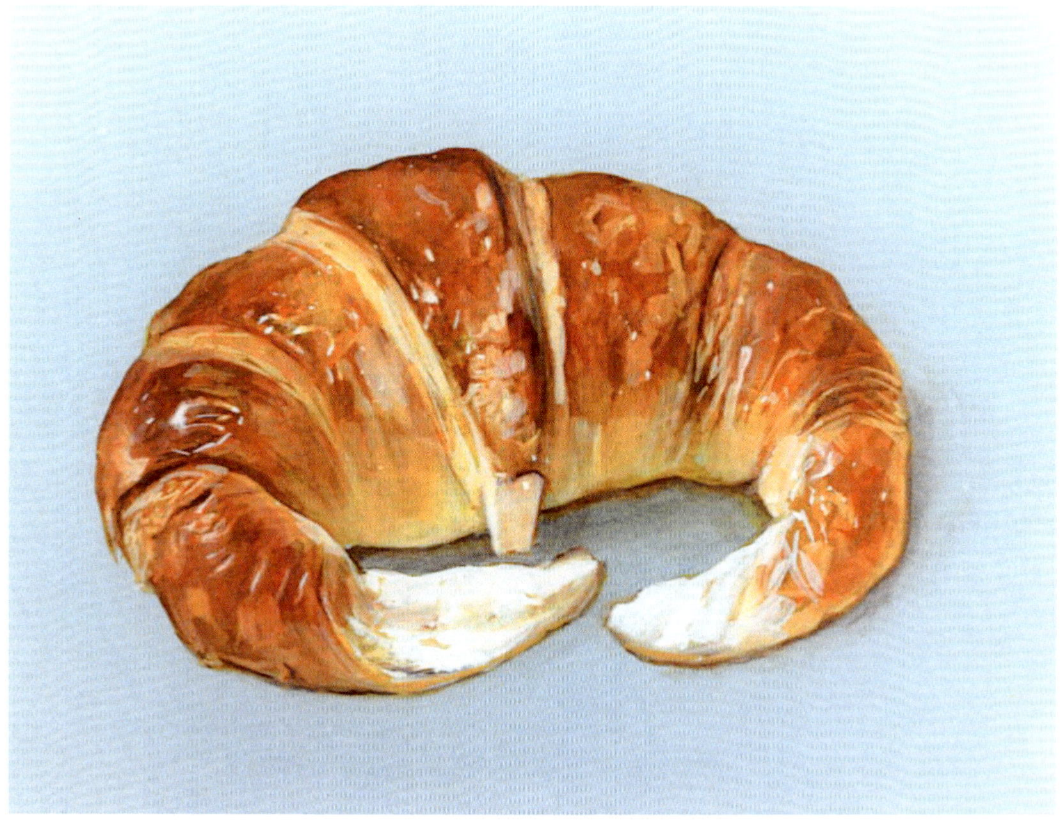

Croissant 1980
Watercolour and gouache on Ingres board 7″ x 11″
Private Collection

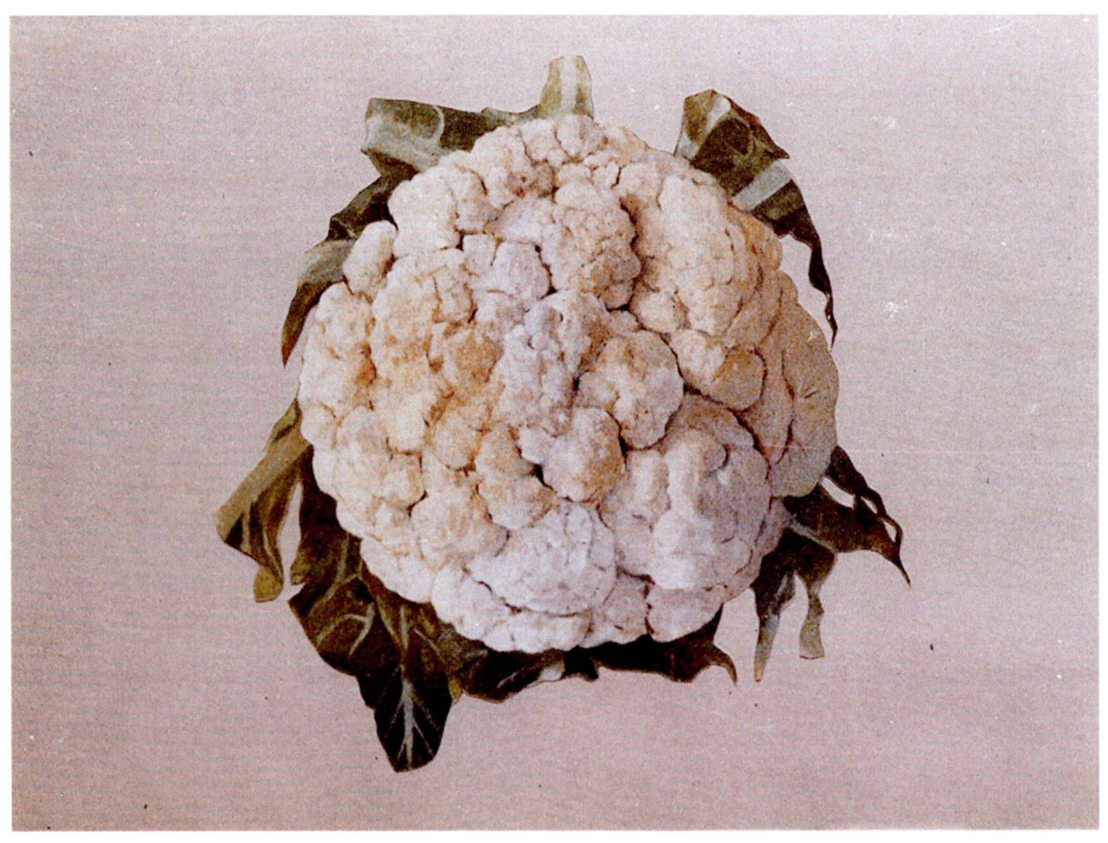

Cauliflower 1979
Oil on linen 48″ x 48″
Private Collection

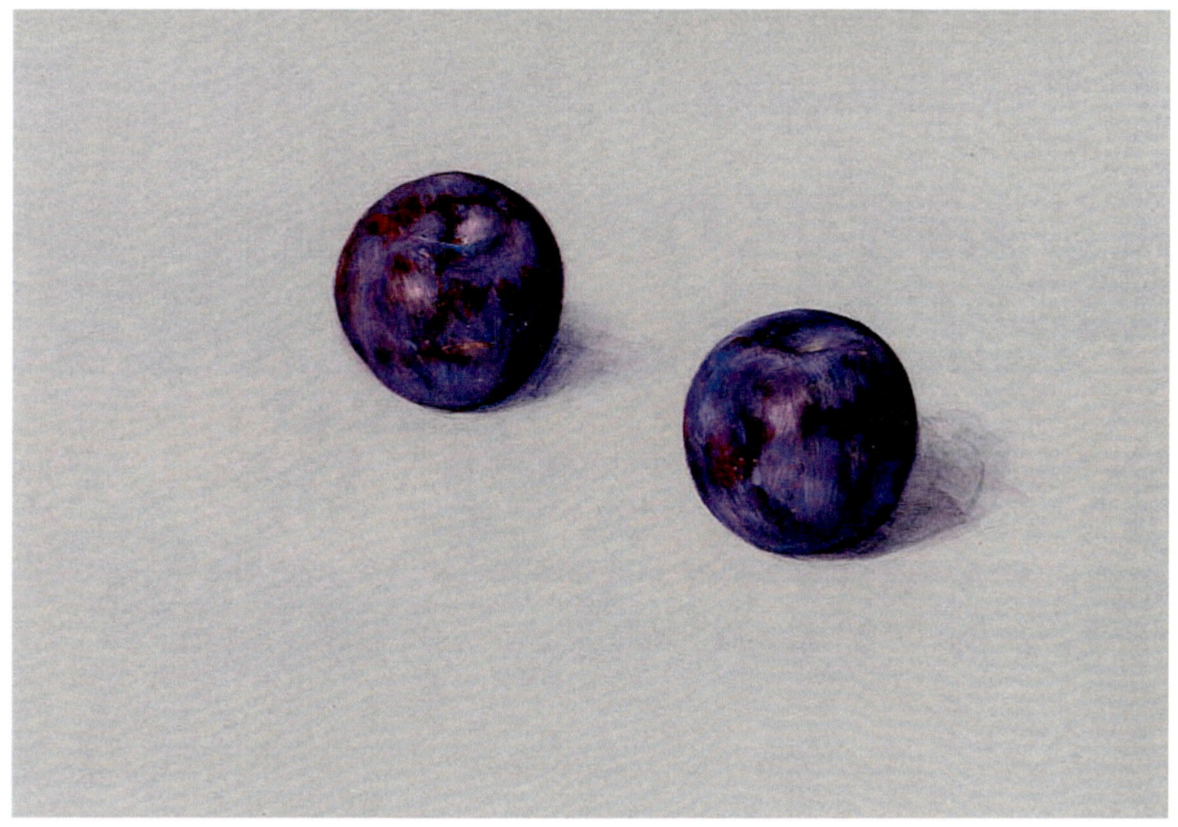

Plums 1980
Watercolour and gouache on Ingres board 7″ x 11″
Private Collection

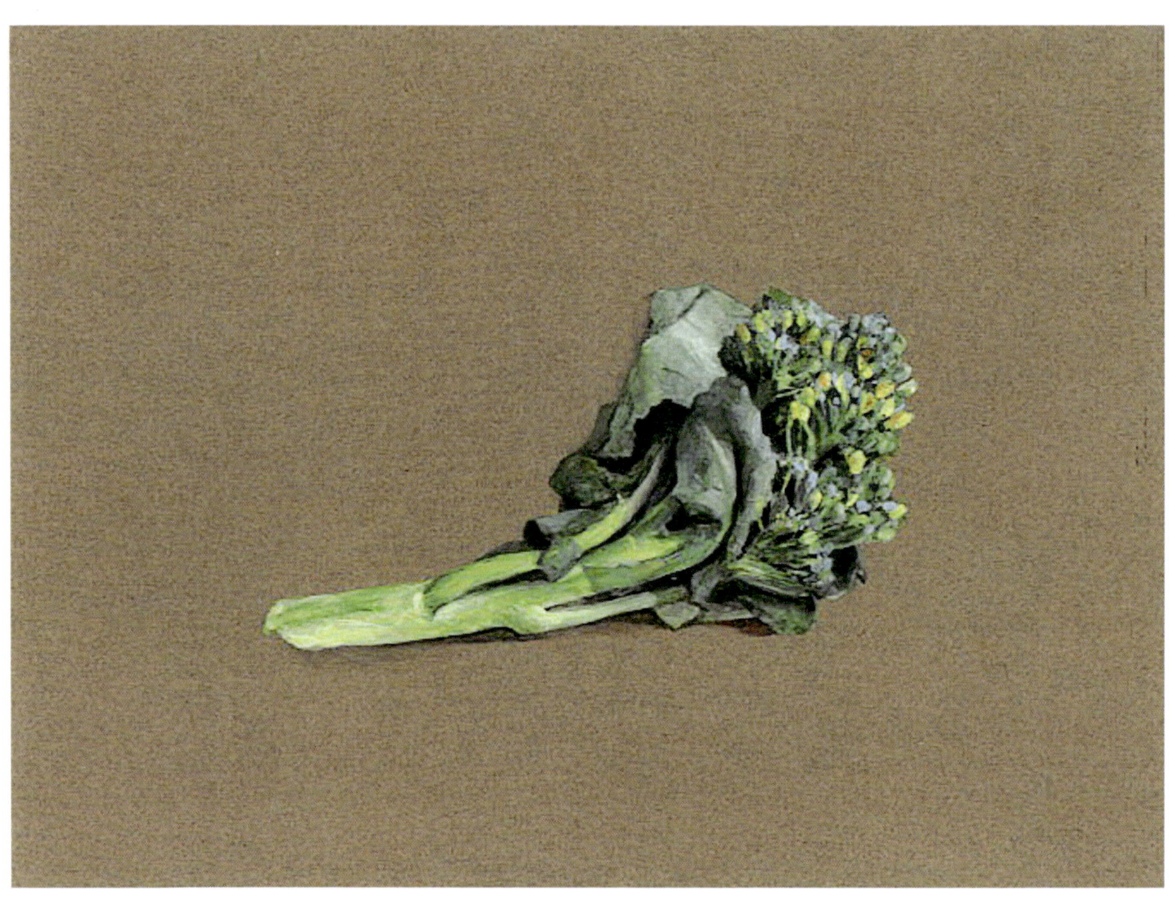

Broccoli 1978
Watercolour and gouache on Ingres board 7″ x 11″
Private Collection

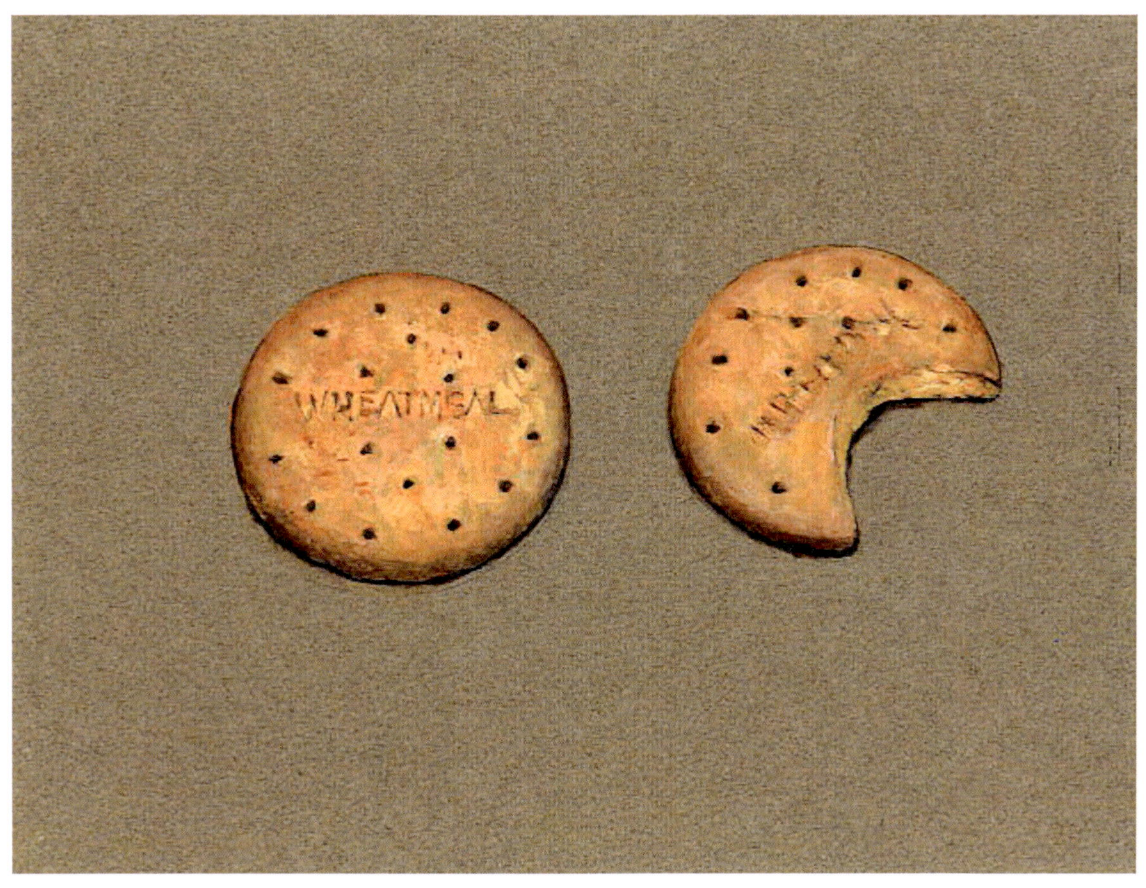

Tea Biscuits 1978
Watercolour and gouache on Ingres board 7″ x 11″
Private Collection

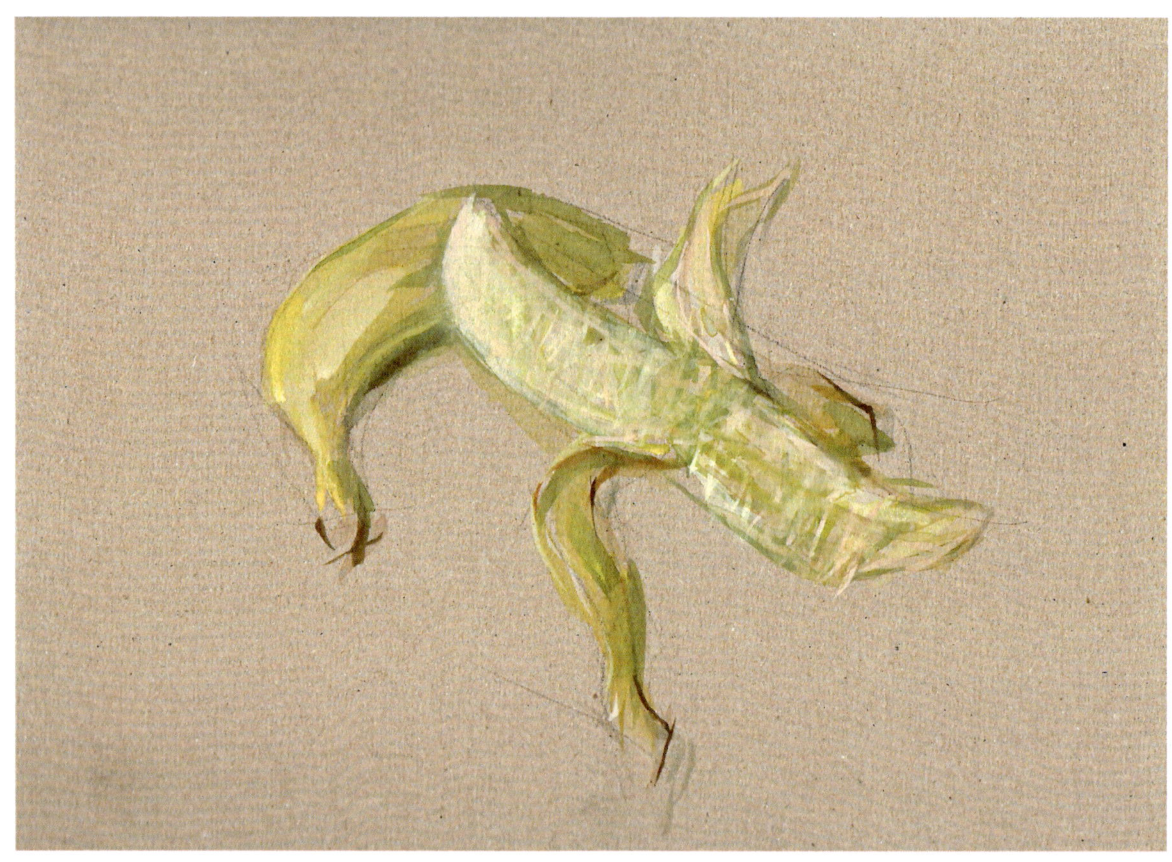

Bananas 2014
Watercolour and gouache on Ingres board 7″ x 11″
Private Collection

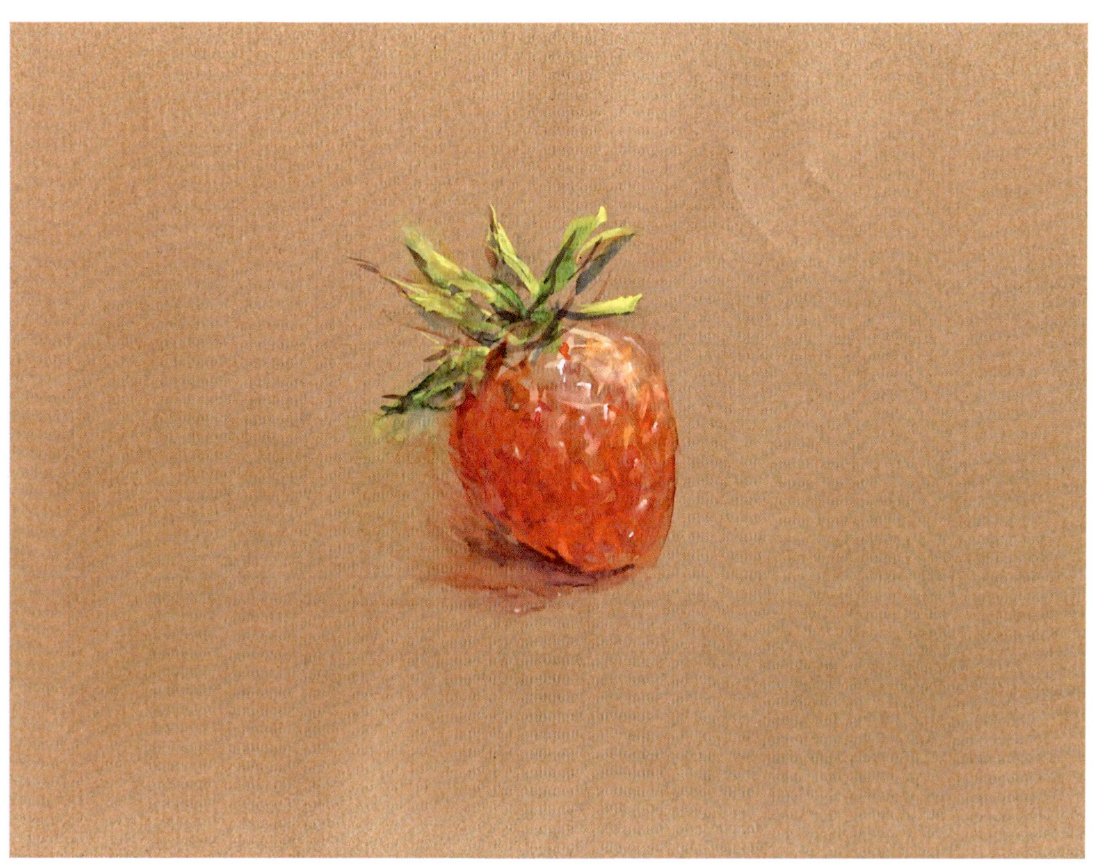

Strawberry
Watercolour and gouache on Ingres board 7″ x 11″
Private Collection

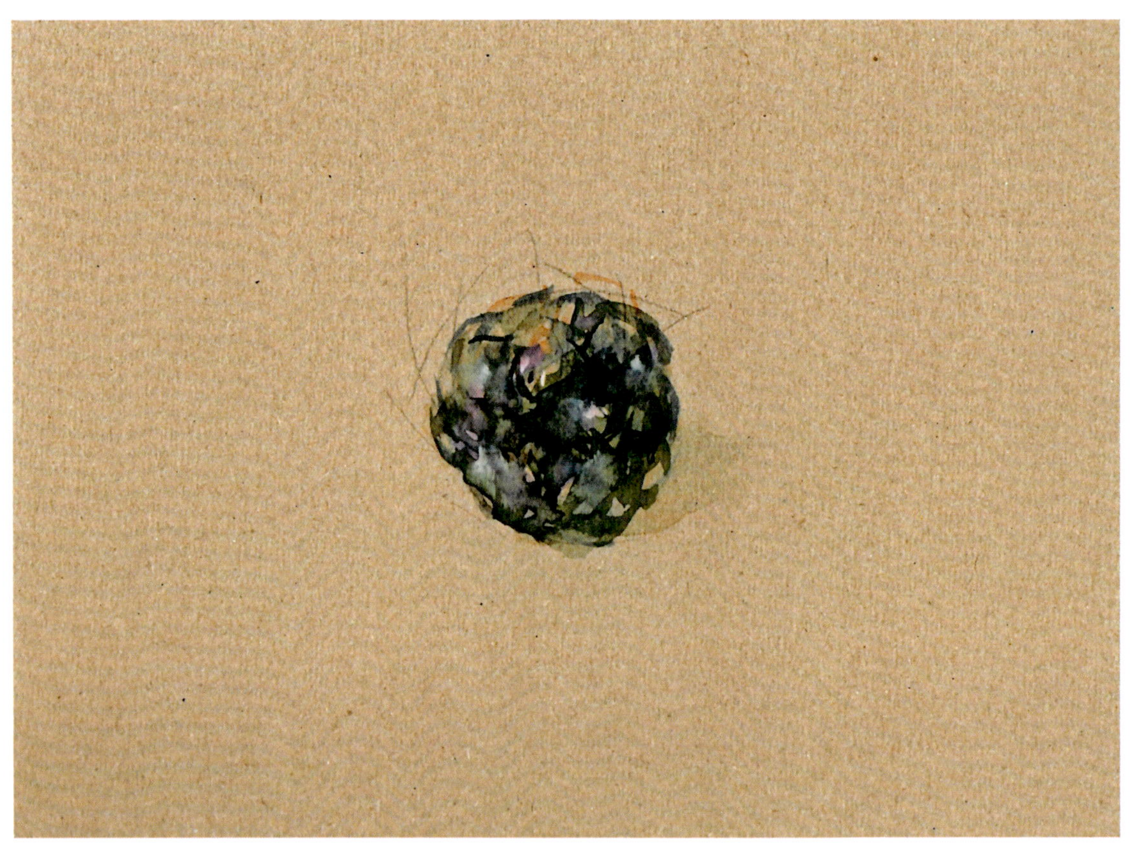

Blackberry 2014
Watercolour and gouache on Ingres board 7″ x 11″

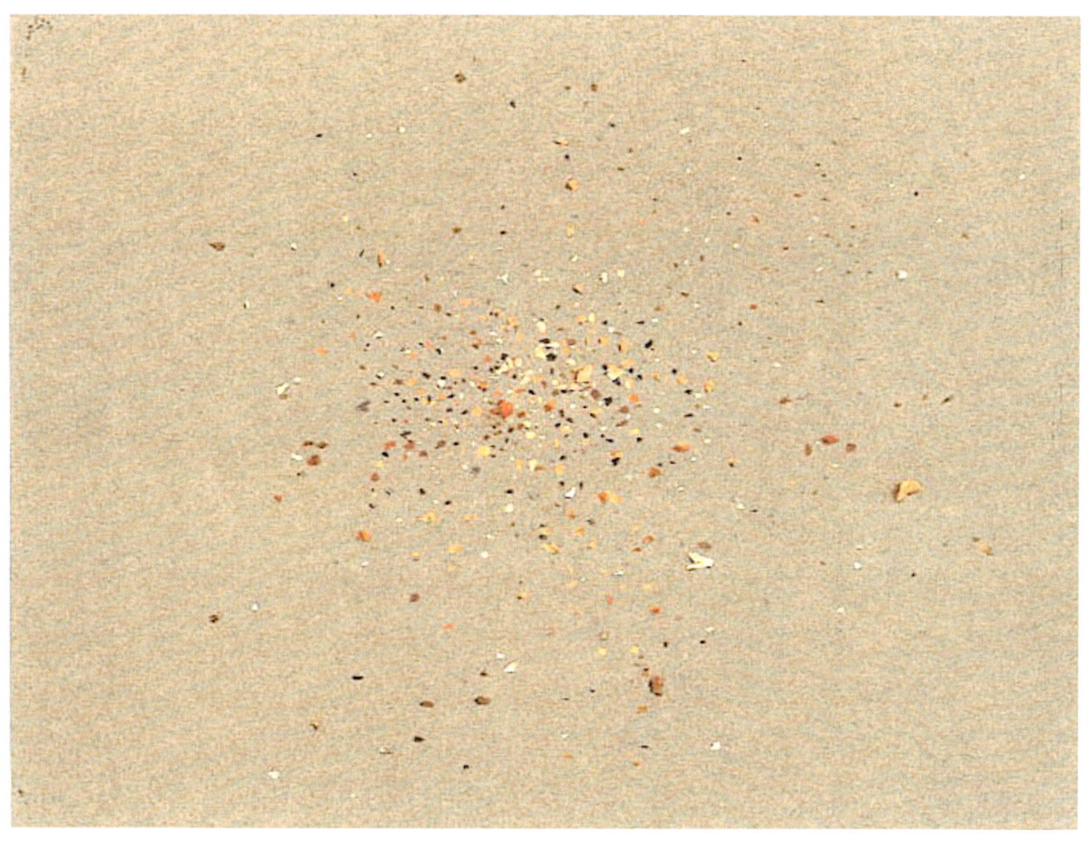

Biscuit Crumbs 1978
Watercolour and gouache on Ingres board 7″ x 11″
Private Collection

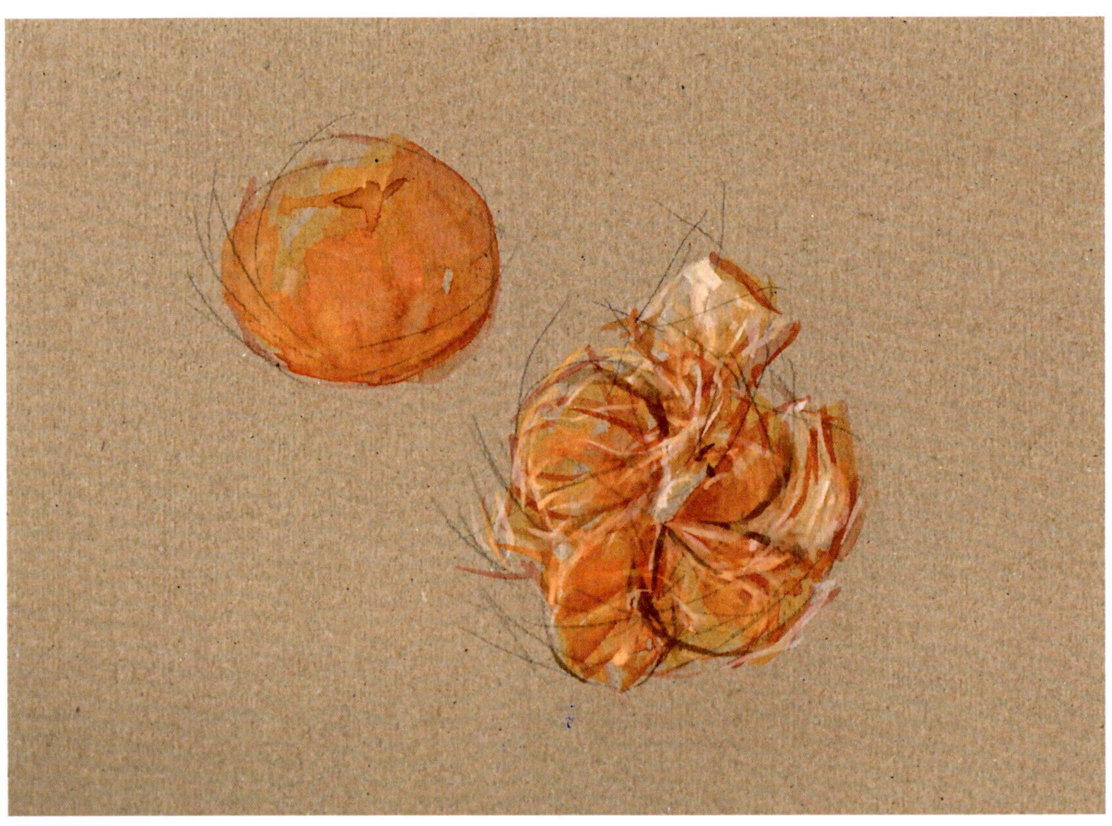

Mandarin Orange 2014
Watercolour and gouache on Ingres board 7″ x 11″
Private Collection

Garlic

A3 landscape format print on 135gsm matt Image centred at 9" x 12", title and credit. Supplied unmounted in roll

GBP 25 per single incl p&p in UK. 3 or more GBP 18 each) p&p quoted at cost inland.. Returns accepted

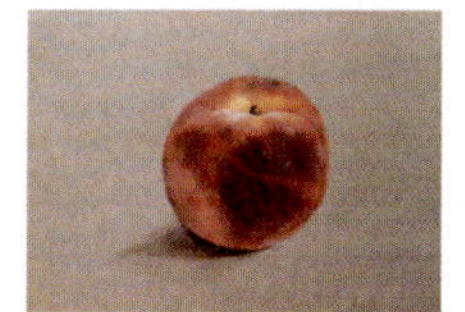

Peach

A3 landscape format print on 135gsm matt Image centred at 9" x 12", title and credit. Supplied unmounted in roll

GBP 25 per single incl p&p in UK. 3 or more GBP 18 each) p&p quoted at cost inland.. Returns accepted

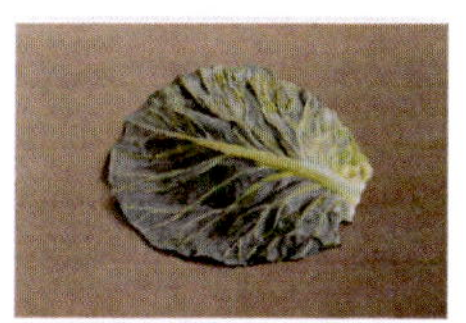

Cabbage Leaf

A3 landscape format print on 135gsm matt Image centred at 9" x 12", title and credit. Supplied unmounted in roll

GBP 25 per single incl p&p in UK. 3 or more GBP 18 each) p&p quoted at cost inland.. Returns accepted

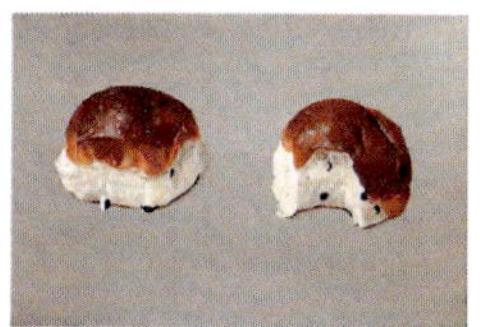

Buns

A3 landscape format print on 135gsm matt Image centred at 9" x 12", title and credit. Supplied unmounted in roll

GBP 25 per single incl p&p in UK. 3 or more GBP 18 each) p&p quoted at cost inland.. Returns accepted

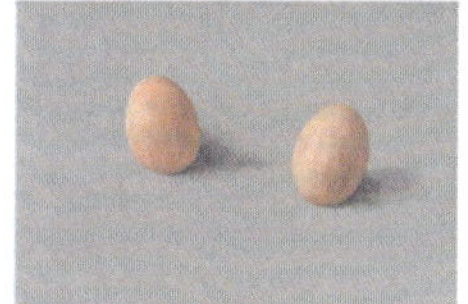

Eggs

A3 landscape format print on 135gsm matt Image centred at 9" x 12", title and credit. Supplied unmounted in roll

GBP 25 per single incl p&p in UK. 3 or more GBP 18 each) p&p quoted at cost inland.. Returns accepted

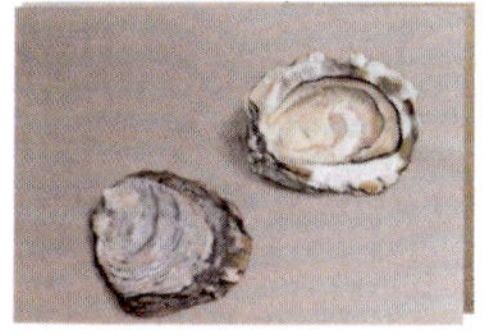

Oyster

A3 landscape format print on 135gsm matt Image centred at 9" x 12", title and credit. Supplied unmounted in roll

GBP 25 per single incl p&p in UK. 3 or more GBP 18 each) p&p quoted at cost inland.. Returns accepted

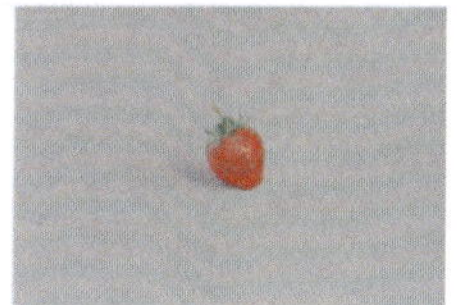

Strawberry

A3 landscape format print on 135gsm matt Image centred at 9" x 12", title and credit. Supplied unmounted in roll

GBP 25 per single incl p&p in UK. 3 or more GBP 18 each) p&p quoted at cost inland.. Returns accepted

Please supply   1/3/6 or more prints of yhe following subjects:
Garlic . Peach . Cabbage Leaf . Buns . Eggs . Oyster . Strawberry .

Name/Address/Post Code/Tel

Pro-forma nvoice against order: prayment by cheque to Cv Publications, mail: Albion House, 49 Park Road, Hampton Wick Surrey UK KT1 4AS. Via paypal email n.p.james@gmx.com

View of the City

Studies of the Square Mile

N.P. James ROI

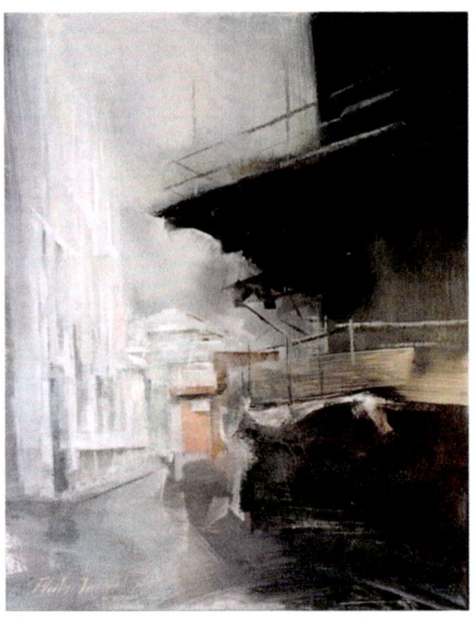

Cv/Visual Arts Research Series 202

ISBN 978-1-910110-16-4

Figure to Ground

The Model Seen and Imagined

N.P. James ROI

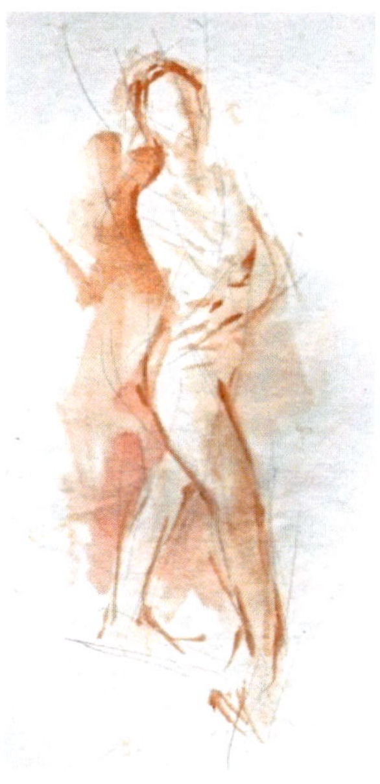

Cv/Visual Arts Research Series 203

ISBN 978-1-910110-17-1

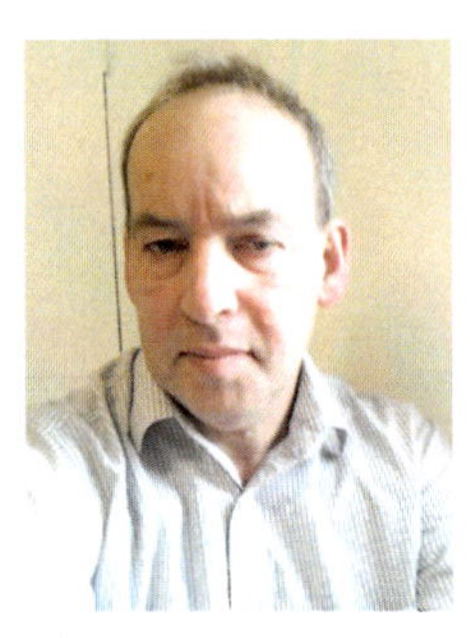

Born November 1948, Bromley Kent Nicholas Philip James studied painting with Frank Auerbach and Keith Vaughan at the Slade School, UCL (BA), printmaking with Stanley Jones at the Curwen Press and History of Art (MA) at Kingston University. His primary attraction to landscape developed in works made in the 1960s on site in Sussex, Devon, Cornwall and the Lake District progressing to city views of London and Paris.

He regularly exhibits at The Royal Institute of Oil Painters (Winsor & Newton Prize 2003, elected a full member 2006). He has shown at Wold Galleries, Gloucestershire, Courcoux and Courcoux, Stockbridge, Hants, The Turner Gallery, Exeter, and Whittington Fine Art Henley, and in April 2008 with his sister Liz Summers at Peter Pears Gallery Aldeburgh, Suffolk,. Forthcoming exhibitions include the RAC Club (December) and Lime Tree Gallery Bristol (ROI Group) Autumn 2014.

The artist's prints are included inthe Tate Britain archive (Curwen Gift) with publications on deposit with The British Library's media and book collections. His work is held in numerous private collections here and abroad. Entries include Dartmoor Artists (Brian Le Messurier, Hallsgrove Press) and Who's Who In Art (Hilmarton Manor Press).   He is publisher and series editor of Cv/VAR Archive and Editions.

Enquiries:
Liberty Rowley ,Emma Wright,
Commissions Consultants,
The Federation of British Artists,
The Mall Galleries, London SW1
020 7930 6844